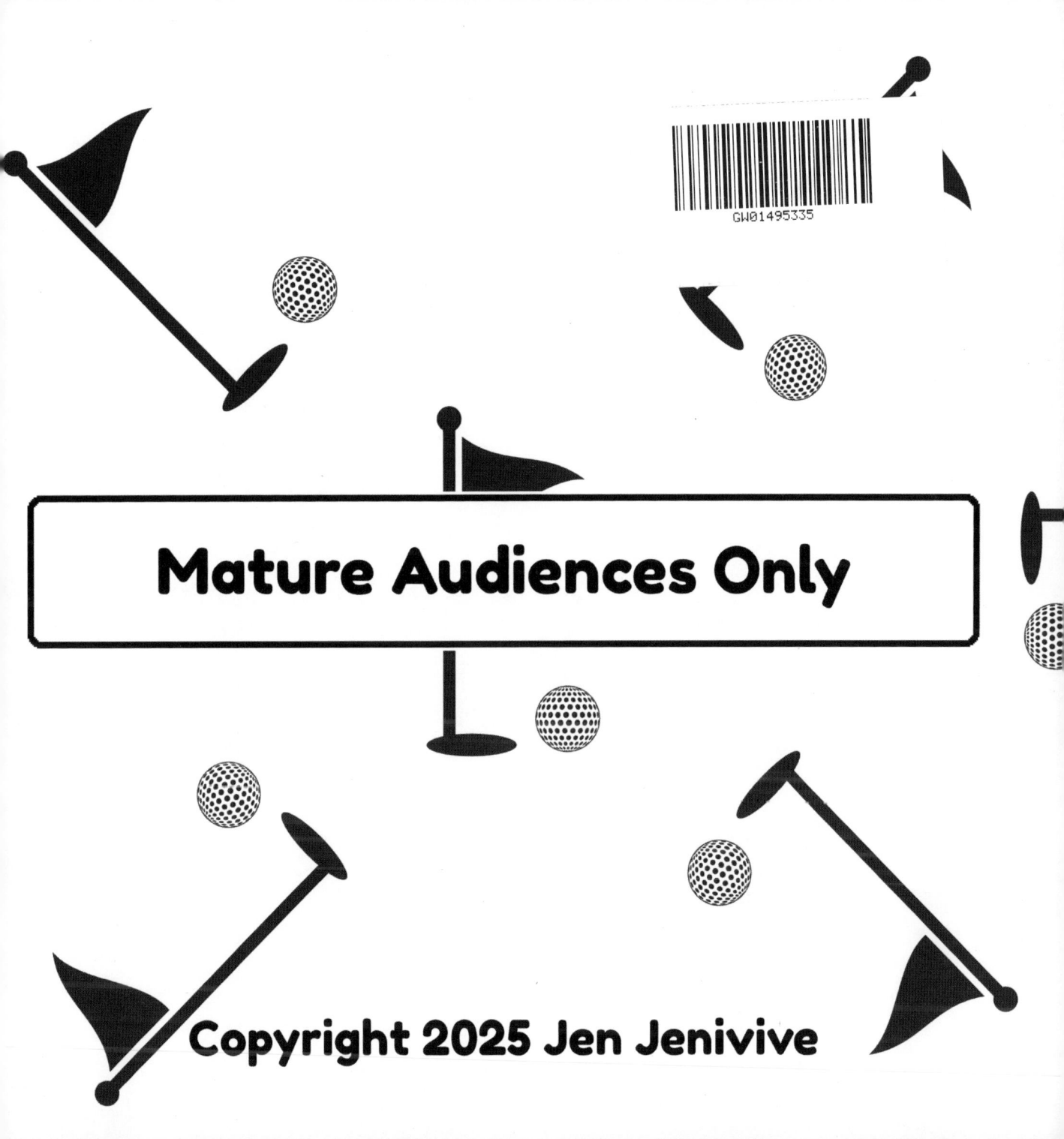

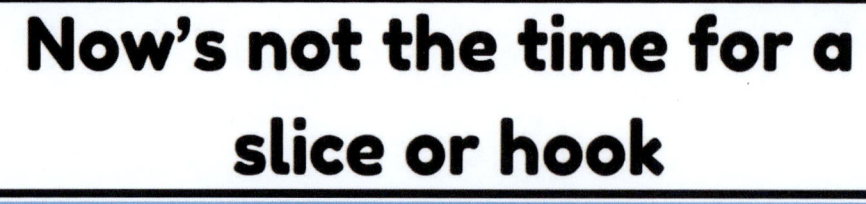

The journey can be full of dangers

WARNING

TIGHT HOLES AHEAD ENTER WITH CAUTION!

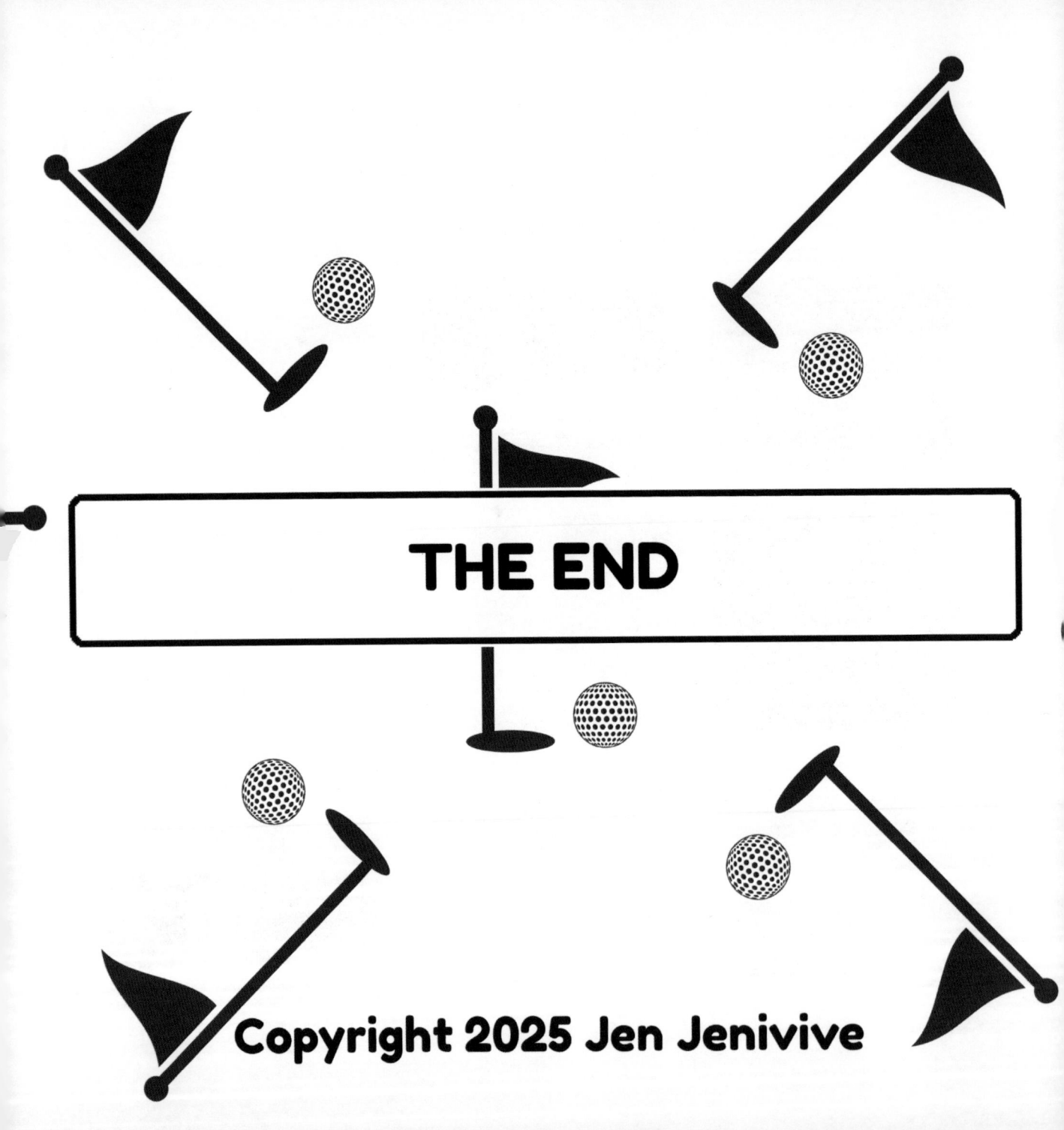

About The Author
Jen Jenivive

Has a glorious hole
Lover of silly, immature humour

 @jenjenivivereads

 @jenjenivivereads

 @jenjenivive

www.jenjenivive.com

Other Titles Include:
For full book collection and signed books visit
www.jenjenivive.com

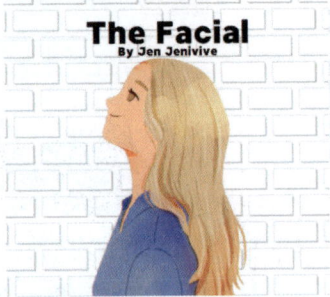  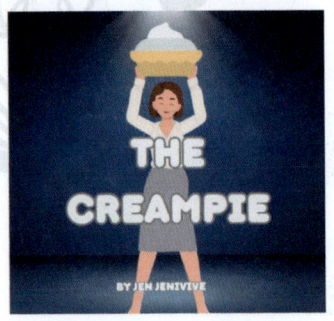
 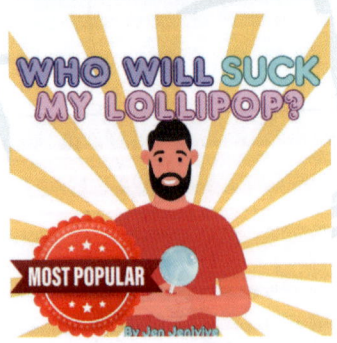 

DID YOU KNOW..?

YOU CAN PURCHASE SIGNED COPIES OF ANY OF MY BOOKS! THEY CAN COME WITH A PERSONAL MESSAGE TOO! PRETTY COOL ISN'T IT?

HEAD TO MY WEBSITE AND USE THE CODE 'WELCOME20' FOR 20% OFF YOUR FIRST PURCHASE!

www.jenjenivive.com

Printed in Dunstable, United Kingdom